Twinkle, Twinkle, Little Star

BY Jane Taylor

ILLUSTRATED BY Michael Hague

Books of Wonder   Morrow Junior Books   New York

Twinkle, twinkle, little star,

How I wonder what you are!

Up above the world so high,

Like a diamond in the sky.

When the blazing sun is gone,

When he nothing shines upon,

Then you show your little light,

Twinkle, twinkle, all the night.

Then the traveler in the dark,

Thanks you for your tiny spark!

He could not see which way to go,

If you did not twinkle so.

In the dark blue sky you keep,

And often through my curtains peep,

For you never shut your eye,

Till the sun is in the sky.

As your bright and tiny spark

Lights the traveler in the dark,

"Twinkle, Twinkle, Little Star" was originally published in 1806 as "The Star" in *Rhymes for the Nursery*, a book of poetry by Jane Taylor and her sister, Ann. It was such a favorite with children and adults that its first stanza soon became a well-known nursery rhyme. Today it is a rare child who cannot recite it by heart.

To Fred and Caroline

Illustrations copyright © 1992 by Michael Hague
Author's note copyright © 1992 by Peter Glassman

Printed in the United States of America.

1 3 5 7 9 10 8 6 4 2

Library of Congress Cataloging-in-Publication Data

Taylor, Jane, 1783–1824.
Twinkle, twinkle, little star / by Jane Taylor; illustrated by Michael Hague.
p. cm.
Summary: An illustrated edition of the familiar nineteenth-century poem celebrating one bright little star.
ISBN 0-688-11168-8
ISBN 0-688-11169-6 (lib. bdg.)
1. Stars—Juvenile poetry. 2. Children's poetry, English.
[1. Stars—Poetry. 2. English poetry.] I. Hague, Michael, ill. II. Title.
PR 5549.T2T87 1992b
821'.7—dc20 92-4216
CIP AC

Watercolors and pen and ink were used for the full-color art.
The text type is 24-point Cochin Bold.

Book design by Marc Cheshire